T0079911

The Art of Good Manners

Bodleian Library
UNIVERSITY OF OXFORD

This edition first published in 2014 by the Bodleian Library,
Broad Street, Oxford, OX1 3BG
www.bodleianbookshop.co.uk

ISBN: 978 1 85124 398 3

Cover design by Dot Little
Designed and typeset by JCS Publishing Services Ltd in 10.75
on 13.75 pt Electra font
Printed and bound in China by C&C Offset Printing Co. Ltd
on 100gsm YuLong pure 1.3 paper
British Library Catalogue in Publishing Data
A CIP record of this publication is available from the British
Library

Contents

TO
W. H. VINEY
A FINE GENTLEMAN AND A FAITHFUL
FRIEND

Introduction

THE true meaning of etiquette can hardly be described in dictionary parlance; it embraces the whole gamut of good manners, good breeding, and true politeness. Some people read everything that is written on the subject of manners, not only those who are ignorant and wish to learn something of its laws, but those who are thoroughly well versed in them and who, one might suppose, had nothing to learn: still these latter like to see what is written, to feel the satisfaction of being supposed in their own knowledge by a well-informed writer; or of finding amusement in the absurdities gravely advanced by someone writing from another sphere than that where savoir vivre reigns. Others attach a very narrow meaning to the word etiquette, and neither accept it nor understand it in its true sense; they have an idea that its rules influence and govern society in general. Rules of etiquette are from their point of view but trammels and shackles; let them be cast off or burst through, say they; let every one do as he likes; let all behave as they like; we are in a free country, why should we not wipe our mouths upon the tablecloth if we please. Others again, devour books of etiquette on the quiet;

they are very much in want of instruction, but they have not the courage to confess that they are aware of this want, and are trying to pick up some knowledge of this kind to be useful to them; as their aim is to rise in the social scale, they would not let their friends know for worlds about this new study, but they know it, and find that they have improved, that they do not commit as many gaucheries as heretofore; still, they have caught the letter rather than the spirit of etiquette, they have read the rules it prescribes, and act up to them as far as their memories serve them; but they have failed in one essential particular of understanding that courtesy, consideration towards others, and unselfishness, are the sources of true politeness from which etiquette springs.

There is an idea amongst some few people who have mixed little in the world, and moved but in one fixed groove, that the more exalted the sphere, the more perfect the manners. It is needless to attempt to refute such a fallacy as this, for examples of the most perfect manner are to be met with not only amongst those who can boast of long lineage and high birth, but also amongst those who lay claim to neither.

The possession of wealth or of talent is the open sesame to the most refined and cultured circles. The word etiquette is too narrow for all it embraces; it must be viewed in a double light, and be taken from a moral point as well as from a conventional one. A kindly nature, and an unselfish spirit are never wanting in true politeness, but the conventionalities of society give the finish and completeness to the whole, the colour, as it were, to the picture. In some the conventional spirit is uppermost and they have at best but a surface polish. In others, the kindly feelings of the heart are allowed full play, and no act of genuine politeness is omitted or left undone in their intercourse with their fellows, and these graces of kindly politeness linger in the memory, trivial though they may have been, years after one has lost sight of this true gentleman or thorough lady, and one says of him, "what a charming man he was, how courteous and considerate, and how kind!" and of her, "She was the sweetest and prettiest-mannered woman I ever met."

It is only given to the very few to be thoroughly and unaffectedly charming without a shadow of self-consciousness or effort. To assume a would-be charming manner for the moment, with the desire to be unusually pleasing to some one in particular, does not confer the enviable reputation of having a charming manner. It does not sit easy enough to be altogether natural; it conveys the idea of being put on for the occasion, and, like all imitations, it hardly ever pleases and seldom deceives. Etiquette and true politeness would have us go further than this, and our manners of to-day should be our manners of to-morrow, and not variable according to place and persons. The world is quick to note these uncertain demeanours, and every one's measure is readily taken and retained.

The rules of etiquette are indispensable to the smooth working of society at large. Take, for example, the etiquette of precedency, in force both in public and in private: on every public occasion, and in every private circle, precedency steps in to render assistance, and is as necessary in the smallest private circle as in the largest public gathering, because it assigns to every one his or her place as far as claim can be laid to place. Mistakes in the matter of precedency are not only committed by those who have enjoyed few social advantages, but by those also who have had everything in their favour. Young ladies, for instance, when married from the schoolroom, as it were, often make grace mistakes on the question of precedency, if they do not ignore it altogether.

The etiquette of card leaving and that of paying calls are indisputably necessary and only the very ignorant would attempt to gainsay their utility; without these aids to order and method, all intercourse between friends and acquaintances would be uncertain and chaotic; as it is there is little excuse when the right thing is not done, and any departure from the simple rules laid down on these heads, is the best possible proof of the standing, position, and associations of the one at fault.

Any one point of etiquette if brought to the bar of common sense would be pronounced reasonable, proper, and sensible; and there is strictly speaking no question of etiquette that can be described as absurd or ridiculous, arbitrary or tyrannical, and taken collectively, the rules are but social obligations due from one person to another. Why should we not be a well-mannered people? Why should we not be refined, cultivated, and polished in our demeanour and bearing? Why should we not seek to charm if we can? Why should we not cultivate and encourage in ourselves consideration, thoughtfulness, and graciousness towards others in the smallest details of daily life?

Preface

It is a sign of the times that there is a very-large demand for a handy little manual which will present in an easily comprehended and concise form a summary of those points the observance of which constitute a claim to the possession of good manners. With the spread of education the old-fashioned lines which so sharply divided the classes are fast vanishing. And now that there is so little distinction in clothes, all that tends to make or mar is to be seen in manners and heard in speech.

Here it is not possible to offer much that is implied by culture. But it is possible to point out the pitfalls that lie in wait for the unwary, and to show how these may be avoided. Attention to the various points indicated will do much to make the individual who practises the suggestions given presentable and acceptable in any class of society.

Much more could of course be written on the subject. But the golden rule is to be observant. If in doubt at any time, be deliberate, watch carefully and note how well-bred people conduct themselves, and do likewise.

Many of the rules and suggestions almost necessarily take the negative form. In our great schools, which are the training-ground for character and conduct, the new boy frequently gets the simple injunction from one of the elder boys as a deterrent against some course of conduct that is reprehensible, "That isn't done here." In good society, amongst well-mannered people, there are *many things that are not done*. It is to point out the principal of these, which might otherwise escape attention, that this little book is written.

CHAPTER I

The Value of Good Manners

IT was, if we remember rightly, Lord Macaulay who once said, "Every schoolboy knows", only to discover almost immediately that scarcely any schoolboy knew the matter he had in mind. And so it might be easy to conclude that everybody knows what a gentleman or a lady is, only to find out that very few really do so.

All of us know fairly well that certain things are what no gentleman or lady would do. But it is by no means easy to say just what constitutes a gentleman. Now, this is a very important part of our programme here. For we shall find that nearly all the rules of good manners are dependent upon the single principle that underlies all that we try to convey by the term "gentleman".

No writer, perhaps, has more clearly expressed in a small space so useful a definition of a gentleman as Cardinal Newman, and we make no excuse for quoting here what he says on the subject in the *Idea of a University*:

"It is almost a definition of a gentleman to say that he is one who never inflicts pain. . . . The true gentleman carefully avoids whatever may cause a jar or a jolt in the minds of those with whom he is cast—all clashing of opinion or collision of feeling, all restraint or suspicion, or gloom or resentment; his great concern being to make everyone at their ease and at home. He has his eyes on all his company; he is tender towards the bashful, gentle towards the distant, and merciful towards the absurd; he can recollect to whom he is speaking; he guards against unseasonable allusions, or topics which may irritate; he is seldom prominent in conversation, and never wearisome. He makes light of favours while he does them, and seems to be receiving when he is conferring. He never speaks of himself except when compelled, never defends himself by a mere retort; he has no ears for slander or gossip, is scrupulous in imputing motives to those who interfere with him, and interprets everything for the best. He is never mean or little in his disputes, never takes unfair advantage, or insinuates evil which he dare not say out. From a long-sighted prudence he observes the maxim of the ancient sage, that we should ever conduct ourselves towards our enemy as if he were one day to be our friend. He has too much good sense to be affronted at insults, he is too well employed to remember injuries, and too indolent to bear malice. He is patient, forbearing, and resigned, on philosophical principles; he submits to pain because it is inevitable, to bereavement because it is irreparable, and to death because it is his destiny. If he engages in controversy of any kind, his disciplined intellect preserves him from the blundering discourtesy of better, though less-educated minds, who, like blunt weapons, tear and hack instead of cutting clean, who mistake the point of argument, waste their strength on trifles, misconceive their adversary, and leave the question more involved than they find it. He may be right or wrong in his opinion, but he is too clear-headed to be unjust; he is simple as he is forcible, and as brief as he is decisive. Nowhere shall we find greater candour, consideration, indulgence; he throws himself into the minds of his opponents, he accounts for their mistakes. He knows the weakness of human reason as well as its strength, its province, and its limits. If he is an unbeliever, he will be too profound and large-minded to ridicule religion or to act against it; he is too wise to be a dogmatist or fanatic in his infidelity. He respects piety and devotion; he even supports institutions as venerable, beautiful, or useful, to which he does not assent; he honours the ministers of religion, and he is contented to decline its mysteries without assailing or denouncing them. He is a friend of religious toleration, and that, not only because his philosophy has taught him to look on all forms of faith with an impartial eye, but also from the gentleness and effeminacy of feeling which is the attendant on civilisation. . . ."

Now, if we try to sum up the matter more concisely, we shall find that "being a gentleman" means showing consideration to others. It is the modern paraphrase of loving one's neighbour as oneself.

Nearly every custom that is necessary in the acquisition of good manners arises from this idea of consideration for others. Politeness, which is one of the hall-marks of good manners, has almost necessarily as its sole basis this consideration for, and regard to, the feelings and desires of others.

And this is so however we analyse the general proposition. If it be in speech, we find that the origin of customs that are reckoned correct are for the purpose of making oneself more easily understood. This is an instance of feeling that we do not wish to put others to the inconvenience of having to try to understand something that is obscure.

A word ill pronounced, sounded wrongly, or accented wrongly, makes it difficult for another to grasp one's meaning at once. An aspirate misplaced or omitted has the same effect. A phrase or a sentence ill constructed, or the use of words that are not current in good society, makes our meaning less clear.

At table, the observance of certain little formalities, to be detailed at length later, makes intercourse more pleasant. It shows plainly that one considers the feelings of others, who themselves do not do those things that are not good form. In the home, in the street, in public places, it is the same. Feeling and consideration for others is *the* principle which should guide us.

Courtesy and consideration draw good dividends. For as like begets like, a little consideration for another will always cause that other to respond. It naturally follows that in good society, where this general rule holds first place, there is an ease and a dignity of behaviour that makes everything seem gracious and polished.

Good taste, which is an evidence of good manners, is shown in dress. It is out of consideration for others and their feelings that we conform to certain customs of attire. Each particular occasion calls for its special variation of costume, and at no time should we go dressed with a lavishness of display of costume or of jewellery that would indicate a desire to shine at the expense of others. One should dress well, which means simply even if expensively.

In order to make this little book the more valuable, it has been divided first of all into chapters, each dealing with some general phase of the application of good manners. Then each chapter is subdivided under headings, bringing together a number of points under each. This will enable those who desire to do so to omit any portions on which they know they are well informed and need no instruction. It will also enable them to find out just those things on which they need information and advice.

CHAPTER II

Manners in the Home and at the Table

IT is often thought that the little courtesies one shows to one's acquaintances need not be cultivated and practised at home. But consideration there is just as necessary as elsewhere. It is an offence against good manners when one is a guest to be late to dinner. At home equally it is so, for irregularity does not promote good feeling in the domestic circle. One always should be properly dressed for a meal. To come to table in *deshabille* is to cast a slight upon others who are present. Do not read at table if others are present. This is a discourtesy. Remain at the table until the meal is quite finished. Always allow ladies to seat themselves before you sit down. If introductions are necessary make them before your guests are seated. Sit easily at the table, neither too close nor too far away.

These few general observations serve to indicate one important point. The observance of good manners is not a garment to be donned for outside use. The man or woman who desires to behave well when out must do so at home also. There cannot be two sets of rules for conduct at home and abroad. Besides, if you may expect to be a guest, you must also expect to be a host.

And the same rules apply all the time. Even if no guests are present, even if you are dining alone, there should be no omissions to mar the general tenor of good and correct behaviour.

Table manners are often considered the most important. This is perhaps because more breaches of the rules are committed at table than elsewhere. We will begin, therefore, with Manners at the Table.

ARRIVAL.—If a guest, always arrive in good time; to do otherwise is a discourtesy to your host, an annoyance and discomfort to the other guests, and an insult to the dinner. If instead of guest you are host, the same rule holds good. You must be prompt to time, and ready to receive the earliest arrival amongst your guests.

PROCEDURE.—In proceeding to the dining-room you should always offer your right arm to the lady appointed to you to take in. If a staircase has to be ascended or descended, allow the lady to take the side next the wall. Your host or hostess will indicate the order in which you should enter the dining-room.

INTRODUCTIONS.—When introductions are essential they should be made before guests are seated.

SITTING DOWN AND RISING.—In the ordinary way, never seat yourself until the ladies have done so. At a formal gathering the host or hostess will give a signal for all to do so. At a signal from the hostess on such occasions the ladies will leave the table first. The gentlemen will stand, and resume their seats only after all the ladies have left the dining-room.

THE NAPKIN.—Spread the napkin easily and handily across the knees. It is not intended to be used as a bib. When necessary to use it, draw it lightly across the lips. It is not intended to be used for wiping or mopping the face. When leaving the table as a guest, the napkin should be placed loosely on the table unfolded, beside your plate. In your own home it is permissible and customary to fold and replace the napkin in the ring. Even at the breakfast-table the napkin is a necessity, though it is often omitted.

BREAD.—Bread should be broken, as required, into convenient pieces. It should not be cut, nor a considerable piece carried to the lips and bitten off. It is not good form to crumble bread into the soup. Soup is a dish intended to be taken as presented. The bread is an accessory to be used as suggested above.

FORK.—At a formal gathering, where a number of courses are to be given, the array of forks often looks formidable. A little quiet thought will soon leave the tyro at his or her ease. There is a perceptible difference usually between the forks for hors d'œuvres, fish, roast, poultry, sweets, and dessert. Usually, too, the arrangement is such that each course finds its own table implements come next in order and nearest to the plate. A safe rule to adopt is that which decrees that a fork shall be used whenever possible in preference to a spoon. Fruit compote or fruit tarts, and even ices, now are eaten with a fork. Do not overload the fork, nor drive it violently into the food. Take up upon it as much as it will carry easily. Approach the mouth with an inward curve. Let the handles of the fork or knife rest in the palm of the hand. Hold them easily but not rigidly. If by chance you should use a wrong fork, make no effort to correct your blunder, and no one will notice it. The servants will replace the fork for its proper course and remove the other. Be self-contained, and, if in any doubt, without apparent hesitation converse for a moment with your neighbour until someone has started. Observe them and do likewise. Do not rest knife or fork with just the points on the plate. Lay them quietly in the plate between the intervals of eating, and when the course is finished, leave them easily together in the centre of the plate. Do not hold knife and fork continually in the hands. The fork when used alone is used in the right hand; otherwise, always in the left hand.

SPOON.—In taking soup use the side of the spoon and carry it easily to the mouth. Avoid any noise in taking the soup either with the mouth or with the spoon in the soup plate. Do not bend over the table as though afraid of losing a drop of the soup. It is permissible to slightly tilt the plate from you to make the effort easier with the latter portion of the soup. Do not endeavour to remove the last spoonful from the plate; there is more food to come. The handle of the spoon should not be held in the palm. The handle should rest easily in the outside of the fork of the thumb, and the middle of the spoon be lightly held between the fore and first finger of the right or left hand. The spoon should be used always in the right hand. Do not leave a spoon in the cup when drinking tea or coffee. It should be allowed to rest in the saucer when not in use to stir the beverage.

KNIFE.—It ought to be unnecessary to have to say, Never put your knife into your mouth; yet this rule is probably the one that is most frequently broken. It is never permissible to eat with the knife. As with forks, so with knives. There is always a distinction between the knives used respectively for fish, roast, poultry, cheese, or dessert. Your knife is your personal implement. It is not permitted to use it for any other purpose. It should not be used to cut the butter in the dish, to take salt, nor to put it into any dish. The spoon or knife that properly belongs to a dish should be used for that purpose only. A butter-knife or a jam-spoon should be used only to remove the necessary portion to your own plate, and then be restored to its proper place.

EATING.—Eat quietly and deliberately. All haste is vulgar; in eating it is particularly so. Make no noise in masticating the food, and keep the mouth closed during the process. Take small quantities of food only into the mouth at the time. It should be possible to talk at any time, because the mouth should never be really full. In taking soup do not gurgle or make throat noises. Do not eat the last morsel of food, nor the last crumb of bread. Eat delicately and not ravenously. It is not usual to desire a second helping from the same dish. This shows distrust of your host's capacity to satisfy your appetite. If it be necessary to return to your plate a piece of bone or other undesirable substance, eject it upon the fork held close to the lips and deposit it quietly upon the plate. Fruit stones should in the same manner be returned to the spoon and placed upon the side of the plate. As host or hostess, see that your own portion is not consumed before that of your guests. If a guest, be in no great hurry to finish your own portion.

DRINKING.—Take wine or other liquor in the same way that you should food—easily, quietly, deliberately, and delicately. Do not elevate the glass as though trying to stand it on your nose. Carry the glass vertically to the mouth, and then incline it gently. Your glass will be filled again when emptied. To drink it quickly is to suggest that you want more. At a formal dinner-party wines will be altered for some of the courses as they follow. Do not be perturbed at the array of glasses. The servants will know the right glass to fill. You have only to follow that lead.

PASSING A COURSE.—In passing a course that you do not care to partake of, do not make remarks about it to your neighbours at table. They are there to enjoy a dinner, not to listen to the possible troubles of your organs of digestion. Simply decline the dish.

CONVERSATION.—The lady sitting next you should receive such conversational attention as you are able to give. Be careful of the subjects you introduce. They should be light and cheerful topics that will make the entertainment more, and not less, enjoyable. Do not lean across one seated next you to talk to another farther away. Do not turn your back to one individual in the process of conversing with another. In conversation, as in eating and drinking, be moderate. A good listener is much more appreciated even than a good talker. Avoid any reference to dietetics or gastronomic processes at table. People are there to eat, not to discuss what happens to the food afterwards.

FIDGETING.—At the table, and elsewhere, avoid fidgeting or fingering articles. Do not play with the table implements or the glasses. Do not crowd the table with your elbows, and do not lounge back in your chair. Sit easily up to the table and remain easily there, turning the head and shoulders only a little left or right in conversation. In eating, keep the elbows close to the body. Your fellow-diners do not want to have personal contact with you.

BLUNDERS.—If you make a blunder—spill your wine, drop a fork or knife—take no notice. A servant will repair the upset or bring a fresh knife. A slip of any other sort will probably pass unnoticed, unless you draw attention to it. You yourself, if you should notice something a little amiss with a fellow-guest, would avoid any attention to it. You would thus exercise the right consideration. Your own little blunders will be as easily passed if you do not force attention upon them by trying to repair them.

DESSERT.—This is sometimes a difficult proceeding. To peel an orange, apple, or pear with fruit knife and fork requires some practice. If you feel doubtful about it, take some other fruit. In eating grapes or muscatels, the stones should be quietly returned to the hand and replaced upon the plate. Bananas should be peeled with the dessert knife and fork and eaten with the fork, which should be used to divide the fruit into small pieces.

SERVICE.—Remember that servants are there to wait. Do not ask a fellow-guest to pass something if a servant is at hand. Do not lean over the table to reach for anything; ask a servant to pass it.

IN GENERAL.—As host or hostess, do not press food upon your guests. It is now considered in bad form to repeat an invitation to take more food. The refusal of the guest is a courteous indication that he has already been well served. At table, even at home in the family circle, do nothing that would be considered bad form when dining out. Humming a tune, whistling a tune, reading a book, a paper, or a letter even, at the table is not good form. An urgent letter or note telegram may be read if permission be first asked of your host, or of the head of the house. Avoid eating onions or any similarly strong-smelling food, unless you intend for some hours afterwards to be eating alone and mainly in your own company. A glass of milk taken after eating onions will help to remove the unpleasant odour.

SELF-POSSESSION.—If you will remember to think mainly of pleasing others, and try to think as little as possible about yourself, you will find traces of embarrassment leaving you. Have respect for yourself, and others will show respect for you. In good society, where good manners prevail, it is easy to be self-possessed, because of the consideration shown by each to the others.

CHAPTER III

In Society

CALLING.—If you make a call and enter a drawing-room, leave your overcoat and umbrella in the hall. If you propose to stay only for a short time, your hat and stick may be carried in the hand. Gloves should not be removed when making an afternoon call.

SHAKING HANDS.—Your host or hostess will welcome you with a handshake. It is not desirable to shake hands when introduced to others present. In any case, it is better to leave to others the initiative. With ladies a gentleman never offers to shake hands. It is the privilege of the lady on all occasions to make the first move. This is an invariable rule. On entering the drawing-room it is sufficient to bow to the company assembled and to address yourself immediately to your host or hostess.

DRESS.—Always dress quietly and unostentatiously. A gentleman should never wear jewellery or rings in excess. This is an offence against good taste. A signet-ring may be worn, and, as is sometimes now the case, a wedding-ring as well. But diamonds are not considered good form. A plain albert may be worn and a simple tiepin. Anything beyond this tends to savour of vulgarity. A lady is permitted more licence. She may wear some jewellery. But this should always be artistic in design, moderate in quantity, and not of a kind to attract attention to itself.

DEPORTMENT.—You may well await an invitation to be seated. Avoid haste or bustle in crossing the room. Be deliberate and self-possessed. You may rest assured that others are not watching you; they have something else to occupy their minds. Be as considerate as they are. Avoid staring at people or things in the room. If your hostess desires you to pay attention to her pictures and furniture, she will ask your opinion about them. Avoid haste in speech or action. A quiet, easy manner is always in good taste. Whatever you do, avoid gush and sentimentality. At the same time, be interested in what is going on, and not affect a cold, distant, and uninterested attitude. When a lady enters the room or leaves it, rise. Be reposeful when seated. Sit in the chair as it is intended you should sit in it—in the middle.

INTRODUCTIONS IN SOCIETY.—In making an introduction, a gentleman, even if of superior rank, should always be presented to the lady. In introducing those of the same sex, the younger should be presented to the elder. It is usually desirable at more elaborate functions to ask permission of a lady to whom you desire to introduce a gentleman. After an introduction the gentleman on a future occasion must always await the lady's signal of acknowledgment. He must not presume upon the fact of a prior introduction to attempt to begin an acquaintanceship.

ASSURANCE.—Endeavour always to be at your ease in whatever company you may find yourself. You will soon see that everyone else is doing the same. They are not bothering about what you are doing, or not doing, or about what you are thinking. They try to please by thinking of others and acting for the convenience and comfort of others. Do the same, and you will find that your self-consciousness will vanish, and that little difficulties will no longer appear.

But do not in your endeavour to cultivate assurance let it tend towards aggressiveness. Be gentle, courteous, self-possessed, cool, and attentive to others.

CONVERSATION.—In this there are numerous pitfalls for the unwary. Let your conversation be light and pleasant. Avoid the appearance of dogmatism. If your opinion be asked, express it freely and easily as your opinion, but pay the same courtesy of listening to the opinion of others. Never contradict; this is an open violation of good form. If the matter be important, you can convey your dissent in an easy, agreeable fashion.

Do not introduce personalities. Avoid the discussion of little things that do not matter really one way or the other. There are plenty of things—music, art, literature, the drama, sport, pastimes—that afford a good ground for conversation without difficulties or dangers. The weather is a little played out. Cultivate most assiduously the art of interested listening. You will be always welcomed as good company if you listen well. But do not forget that you should on occasions be able at least to start an interesting subject.

SCANDAL.—You have already been cautioned against personalities. These usually take the form of scandal. Scandal, though dearly loved by some persons, is really in the worst possible taste. If you consider a fair method of dealing, it would be to say nothing behind a person's back that you would not relish saying to them face to face. This is a safe rule. Follow it always, and you will not go far wrong.

ARGUMENT.—Discussion is always allowable, but argument is better left alone in society. Since the first rule is to allow to every other person the same freedom that one claims for oneself, any attempt to browbeat or to impose one's own opinion upon others is in bad taste. Deliberate discussion in which one airs one's views is another matter. It is then not a question of debate, of answering another's points, of attempting to prove those points wrong, so much as a light and graceful effort to illuminate a topic from various points of view, all of which may differ, whilst all are true as so seen.

BOREDOM.—It often happens that one is bored. When this occurs, do your best to disguise your feelings. It is not considered good form to betray your feelings openly. The bore, probably with the best intention, is doing his best to interest you. Let his example be a warning to you. Study his weak points and zealously avoid them in yourself.

ENTERTAINMENT.—When you are asked out, an effort will be made to entertain you. It is your duty not only to appreciate the efforts made, but to reciprocate them. You must appear not only to value the attentions paid to you, but, if in your power, do something in return. It may be quite a trivial matter, but your host or hostess will appreciate it. Remember that you are expected to place yourself at the service of others in the same way that they place themselves at yours.

COURTESY.—Always remember the claims to courtesy due to the fair sex and to your elders, If in any doubt, always err on the wrong side. Cross a room to open the door for a lady to leave rather than allow her to open it for herself. Never sit in the presence of a lady who remains standing. Rise always when a lady enters or leaves a room. Be ready to offer a seat to a lady or to one of your elders. To your equals be courteous, but not servile; they are your equals. To your superiors in station you are not expected to fawn; they are human like yourself. To your inferiors be civil and polite. It commands their respect and wins their admiration. To be overbearing to one's inferiors marks a petty spirit and a wholesome fear of one's own position.

CONCEIT.—Avoid the capital I. If you are really as important as you think you are, you will be soon found out. If not, and you insist upon it, your drop will be the greater. Remember that others, although they good-naturedly may appear to be, are not nearly so interested in yourself as you are. Do not therefore draw attention to yourself and to what you can do, or have done; there are other topics even more important and much more worthy.

TRAVEL.—If you have travelled, do not make it too apparent, for the reasons given above. A casual allusion may be allowed to pass. And if interest be shown and questions are asked, you may equally casually impart a little of your knowledge. But remember, when you do so, that it is at least probable that you have been asked because they desire to show you consideration. Do not wait for danger-signals of boredom from the others, but lightly switch off the conversation to other topics in which they can talk and you can listen.

PRAISE AND BLAME.—Moderation is the best keynote. Do not be lavish with your praise. This denotes a not too well filled mind. Do not be over-emphatic in your condemnation; nothing shows a smaller mind. If you have cause to praise or to blame, let it be apparent that your opinion is well based and well poised.

INTEREST.—Always let your interest be apparent. Do not in company glance frequently at your watch, as though you were anxious to get away. Do not in company pick up a book to read, and so isolate yourself from the remainder. Do what you can to appear interested and entertained, even if you really feel otherwise. Your host is doing his best, and his efforts call for your appreciation.

DEPARTURE.—Your host and hostess will not indicate perhaps quite plainly to you that it is time to go. Their consideration for you would prohibit this. But your consideration for them should tell you when to go. Do not overstay your welcome. Take the tip from others. It is not necessary to go round the room bidding your fellow-guests good-bye. A general glance and farewell greeting is sufficient. And let this be done in a modest and impersonal way. You must not obtrude upon the others merely because you are going. In bidding good-bye to your host or hostess, shake hands and express your thanks for a good time.

COMMENT.—It is advisable not to comment on your host's appearance or on that of his furniture or pictures. Such as they are, they are the best he can afford, and they should be taken for granted. If he desires your notice of a piece of furniture, an *objet d'art*, or a picture, your opinion will be asked, after your attention has been directed to it.

CHAPTER IV

In Public

WALKING.—In walking in public there are a number of little points that may well be mentioned. If accompanied by a lady, allow her always the inside berth on the pavement. Allow your fellow-pedestrians ample room. If you should stumble against one, apologise. Above all things, do not crowd or push. Avoid staring at those you meet, or turning round to look after those who have passed. Indicate by speech persons or things to which you want to invite attention. Do not point. If you carry a cane or an umbrella, do so in a vertical position, To carry either in a horizontal position, particularly if tucked up under the arm, is to invite accidents.

TALKING.—When in the street or the train, do not raise your voice as though to invite everyone within hailing distance to listen. But do not, because you are in a public place—the street or train, for example—lower your voice to a whisper, as though you dreaded to be overheard. A well-bred individual in public talks quite naturally to the one to whom he addresses his remarks, as though no others were present. If there are, and they are equally well-bred, they are concerned with their own matters only. At the theatre or a concert, if you must talk, do so between the acts or the numbers. The others present pay to hear the performers, not yourself.

EATING.—The proper place to eat is at the table. It is inexcusable to be seen in public eating as you walk or travel.

OBSTRUCTIONS.—Be careful to avoid standing in the entrance of a public way, at a railway platform, or the entrance of a public vehicle. Others may want to enter or leave, and you must show them the same consideration that you desire for yourself. If in a crowd, resist the pressure if pushing is indulged in. Make way always for a lady in a crowd, even if you yourself lose your place by it.

SMOKING.—If you are smoking in public, be careful that the smoke shall not be offensive to others. Cigar smoke is sometimes very acrid to those who do not smoke. If walking with a lady, ask her permission before you smoke, and see that she is sheltered from the fumes. When standing still in a public place, a theatre vestibule, or the promenade of a concert hall, or at a railway station, great care should be exercised to avoid annoyance in this way. Never enter a friend's house smoking. If approaching a lady friend who may stop you, see that you are prepared to terminate your smoking.

GREETINGS.—When you greet your friends in public, let it be done quietly and without ostentation or gush. They will expect you to be pleased to see them, but will not expect you to make a scene. Do not gush or be over-familiar. Exercise restraint and self-control in every direction. Do not stop a business friend in business hours. If you have time to waste, he may not.

ADIEUX.—If you intend to leave a friend, take an opportunity to say so, bid good-bye and go. Nothing is more embarrassing than continually to be told, "I must be going", and no departure following.

FASHION.—Let your good taste, when necessary, override mere fashion. Be well dressed at all times, but not overdressed just to be "it". You may safely leave this to brainless fools of either sex who are incapable of thinking for themselves. There is no occasion to look archaic or dowdy. There is a mean, or middle, course in everything. Avoid extremes in fashion as in all else.

SALUTING.—It ought to be unnecessary to say that a gentleman always removes his hat when it is desirable to acknowledge a lady's salutation. But he should always wait for the lady to intimate her recognition of him. If it is necessary to perform some slight service for a lady with whom he is unacquainted, a gentleman salutes in due form. It may be that he has picked up for her an article dropped, or given her some directions in reply to an inquiry: the hat should be lifted. If accompanied by a lady and you meet a friend, a formal salute is essential in reply to his, which is out of courtesy for your fair companion. So, too, if with male friends, and one of them salutes in passing, your own hat should be lifted. It is not the custom in this country for gentlemen to salute one another, very generally, by lifting hats. But in the case of a junior to one his senior in years or station, it is a courtesy that may well be paid—and acknowledged.

INTRODUCTIONS.—It is not necessary to introduce friends who are accompanying you to any others you meet unless you are assured that such introduction would be agreeable and welcomed by both parties. A casual meeting entails no necessity for further acknowledgment.

HASTE.—All haste and bustle is essentially vulgar. A well-bred individual has time for all things. This apparent leisure and self-possession are the hall-marks of a well-mannered man or woman. But these virtues must not be pushed to excess. Your deliberation and self-assurance must not be allowed to trespass upon the time or upon the consideration of others. It must be your object to make yourself agreeable to them— not tedious.

CHAPTER V

In Everyday Life

DRESS.—A word has been said in another place about the undesirability of being dressed in the extreme fashion. Here a word of caution is considered necessary about dress for special occasions. For afternoon calls or garden-parties morning dress is worn—frock-coat or morning-coat and silk hat. Gloves and cane, or umbrella, should be carried. For dances, dinners, or theatres, evening dress should be worn, with silk hat or crush hat. A soft felt *may* be worn if the party is a little informal. For weddings morning dress, with silk hat and rather lighter-coloured trousers than usual, and light gloves. In the country much more freedom is permitted in the way of clothes for ordinary wear. But in making calls or for parties, etc., the rules given above should be followed. It is sometimes the custom on the invitation to indicate a relaxation of the rules for garden-parties of a mixed kind, where boating or tennis, etc., may be indulged. Flannels and soft felt or straw hats are then quite in order.

APPOINTMENTS.—Be careful in making appointments to see that nothing will interfere with your keeping them, and that they are definitely fixed so as to leave no ambiguity on either side. Keep your appointments to the minute. It is the greatest discourtesy to your friends to keep them waiting, since they may have inconvenienced themselves to attend. In business relations this is most important. A business man's time is money; and you have no right to waste another's money.

SERVANTS.—In dealing with servants or inferiors, always exercise sympathy and understanding. Remember that they are of the same material as yourself, with the same desires and needs, emotions and thoughts, which differ in degree only, and not in kind. Remember, too, that they have probably not the advantages that you possess. It should be your place to set them an example and a course of conduct to adopt. Ask kindly, if firmly, for what you want done. Do not be harsh nor unnecessarily curt. Always acknowledge a service done. Thanks cost nothing, but are appreciated by everyone. Whenever you can find an opportunity for saying a kind or encouraging word, do so.

ARROGANCE.—No fault is to be deplored more than arrogance. It is almost universally the mark of an ill-bred individual. It betrays a mistrust of their own position by those who exercise it. The real gentleman or lady is one who takes it for granted that what is required will be done because they have a right to expect it to be done by their method of asking. The service they ask is one that injures the self-respect of no one to render. Instead of a peremptory and haughty "Do this", they will couch a command in the form of a request. And it is not only the form of the words, but the tone of them, that makes them the more acceptable.

FRIENDSHIPS.—An acquaintanceship is easily formed. It should not be allowed too easily to pass into a friendship. The more intimate relationship is one that calls for far greater responsibilities and entails more obligations. Your friend is one whose good name you must guard as you would your own. He is one to whom you have accorded the right to privileges. Do not impose upon your friends your domestic troubles and worries. Your duty to them is to help them and to sweeten their lives. Do not discuss with one friend the failings or short-comings of another. This is a double abuse of friendship. Speak well of others or not at all is a good rule.

BORROWING.—"Neither a lender nor a borrower be." There are many persons to whom it is a delight to share with another the temporary possession of a book, for example. It increases one's joy in the possession of a thing to know that another has enjoyed it also. If, then, a friend lends you a book, be careful to treasure it whilst you have it, and, above all, to return it promptly. Beyond this interchange of books, for this is the best arrangement, there should be little occasion for borrowing and lending. One should value one's independence too highly to have it encroached upon the admission that one is not self-sufficient. Avoid lending money. Never borrow it. If you find a really hard case, give freely to the best of your ability. This closes the cases. Borrowing and lending are always the cause of trouble at some time.

FRANKNESS.—This is a virtue that easily passes into a vice. Be straightforward and honest in the expression of your opinions, but see that you do not inflict annoyance or pain in so doing. It frequently is best to exercise restraint rather than to express quite frankly what one feels. A safe rule is to consider the possible effects of what one is about to do. If it is likely to be hurtful, refrain. There are occasions, however, when it is necessary to be frank, and one should not hesitate then to speak openly if this will avoid misunderstanding or clear up a tangle.

INVITATIONS.—When issuing invitations, let them be very clearly worded. Give a date, time, and period. Do not ask a friend, for example, to come to see you any time convenient to him. This means nothing to him, and he is entitled to believe that it means as little to you. An invitation for a week-end is ambiguous, for it may mean Saturday afternoon until Monday morning or Friday to Tuesday. Make it perfectly clear what you mean: "I shall be pleased if you will come to spend the weekend with me. There is a convenient train from —— Station at 5.30 on Friday which will get you here in good time for dinner. Bring your golf-clubs, racquet, or rods if you prefer to fish. There are plenty of trains on Monday morning, reaching town between ten and eleven. If you cannot manage to run down on the Friday evening, say what time we are to expect you on the Saturday." This leaves nothing in doubt. If the invitation is for a longer period, make it just as definite: "We shall be pleased if you will spend a week (ten days or a fortnight) with us in August. A convenient date for your arrival would be the 8th. We are expecting the ——, whom you know very well," etc. For an informal call, even, there is just the same necessity for precision. "Will you come to meet a few friends on Monday at seven for music and talk on art and literature? We occasionally finish with a game of cards, and break up about twelve. Ordinary dress, of course."

CHAPTER VI

Things for Attention in Speech

IF we examine the reasons for correctness in speech, we find once more that it is because we have consideration for others. We desire to cause them no annoyance or inconvenience by sounds that offend them or make it difficult for them to understand us. The best guide is to listen to well-educated persons and imitate them.

THE ASPIRATE.—One great difficulty that is found is the proper use of the aspirate—the initial letter *h*. When used, it should not be forcibly sounded as though to impress others with your knowledge. Let it be pronounced easily and clearly. A few words beginning with *h* omit the aspirate, as, for example, "heir", "honour", "honest". Others, such as "hotel", "hospital", "humour", and "herb", are occasionally pronounced with the aspirate omitted. Be careful to avoid the use of an aspirate where it does not occur. It sometimes happens that an *h* is sounded as the result of a forced emphasis.

SLANG.—It is difficult to define slang. It is perhaps equally difficult, unless great care be exercised, to avoid its use altogether, as some slang insensibly becomes incorporated with the language. It will help if you always choose simple, easy words. Think first

...arly of what you mean to say, and use those words which cultivated persons would use. Some slang is perhaps permissible. But most of it is merely vulgar. If in doubt, do your best to avoid it altogether.

EJACULATIONS. — Do not use expressions which are practically meaningless or profane: "My hat!" "Oh, lor'!" "Goodness me!" "By Jove!" "What ho!" "Loads of time", and many others which will readily recur if one thinks for a moment.

PRONUNCIATION.—Every word has a proper sound. Make yourself acquainted with its correct sound by looking it up in a dictionary if in doubt. Speak always with a distinct enunciation. Do not clip your words, swallow them, nor smother them. Your purpose is to make yourself understood. Do not impose an unnecessary strain upon your listener. Give each syllable its fair value. Sound letters like r in "arm", "warm", "horse", "government", "Parliament", etc.; like the final g in "singing", "dancing", "skating", etc.; like the w in "window", "fellow", etc. Do not say "sentunce" for "sentence", nor "seperate" for "separate."

ADJECTIVES.—Be moderate in your use of adjectives. If a thing is merely pretty, do not say it is magnificent; do not use the word "awful" except in its proper sense. A thing is awful only when it inspires awe—this does not often happen. A much-abused word is "smart". This has a very limited meaning, and should not be used to convey the idea of cleverness, intelligence, or business capacity. There are very few synonyms—words which have the same meanings. Be sure, therefore, before you speak, of exactly what you wish to convey, and use only that word which most clearly expresses your meaning.

"Me" and "I".—There is often some difficulty as to the correct use of "I" and "me". The one is the nominative case—the other ("me") the objective. The latter is governed by a preposition or a transitive verb. "Between you and me" is correct. "This belongs to you and me", "This is for you and me", etc., are all correct. But where the personal pronoun is the subject, such as "You and I will go to the races", "She and I are going to the theatre", the nominative is always used.

"Who" and "Whom".—The same difficulty is experienced with *who* and *whom*, *she* and *her*, *he* and *him*. The rule should be learned from a grammar, and all the prepositions governing the objective cases, "whom", "her", and "him", committed to memory. "This is the man *to* whom I gave a shilling"; "I *gave* (transitive verb) *her* a shilling also"; "This shilling is *for* him."

"Lie" and "Lay".—A hen may lay an egg or a bricklayer a brick. But one should say to a dog, "Lie down", or "I will lie down." "Lay" is a transitive verb: the action is carried over to an object. It is correct, but not now usual, to say, "I will now lay *me* down to sleep."

"Teach" and "Learn".—"I will teach him, and if he is a good pupil he will learn." One must not say, "I will *learn* him this or that."

"Fewer" and "Less".—Of a number one should say *fewer*: "There were fewer fish to be bought in the market to-day"; "There were fewer visitors yesterday at the exhibition." "We ought to burn less coal," and "We ought to drink less wine," are correct. "Less than a gallon", "Fewer than a dozen", shows the difference.

"Got".—This is a much-abused word. Most sentences are stronger for its admission. "I have *got* an umbrella" is better said as "I have an umbrella."

"What" and "Which".—"The reasons *what* you mentioned" is much better expressed as "The reasons you mentioned"; or, if one wishes to be emphatic, "The reasons *which*", etc.

"Woman" and "Female".—It is not courteous to speak of females. There are females amongst the lower animals. If one wishes to indicate the human being, "girl" or "woman" is correct.

"Lady" and "Gentleman".—And here a word may be said about the indiscriminate use of the words "lady" and "gentleman". In a personal sense, "Show this lady or this gentleman to the door, please," is quite correct; but to speak of one's gentlemen or lady friends is not the best form. Ladies always speak of themselves *generally* as women and gentlemen as men.

"Saw" and "Seen".—To begin with, be careful about the pronunciation of "saw". Do not say *sawr*. "I saw him" is often incorrectly expressed as "I seen him." "I have seen him" is, of course, correct.

"Hung" and "Hanged". — Pictures are hung, but sometimes men are hanged. Do not confuse the two.

"Genteel".—This is a word that no well-bred individual ever uses. Speak of a thing as pleasant or tasteful, or of a person as well-mannered, if this is what you mean to convey.

"Its" and "It's".—"Its" is the possessive form of "it". "Every flower has its own colours" is right. "It's" is a contraction of "it is". "It's a fine day" is not wrong; but it is better to say or to write, in full, "It is a fine day."

CHAPTER VII

What to Cultivate in Correspondence

BREVITY.—In correspondence, above all things, be brief. It is not fair to your friend to waste his or her time in reading a long, rambling description that constantly evades the point. Avoid postscripts. Say what you have to say at once. Be careful, however, to leave no chance of misunderstanding for the reader. Think first of what you wish to say, and then write it.

POST-CARDS.—It is not considered good form to use post-cards for private messages. But there is now some relaxation of the rule. Only unimportant matters that require no answer should be dealt with in this manner. For business uses a post-card is permissible.

STATIONERY.—Always use good quality note-paper and envelopes. This is a mark of refinement, especially if one is careful to avoid any lavish display in colour or ornamentation. Nothing but the address with crest, if one be used, or the writer's monogram should appear on the note-paper.

ADDRESS, FORM OF.—In addressing a married lady, do not use *her* Christian name. She is either Mrs. Smith (for example), if there is only one in your circle of acquaintances; or Mrs. Smith, junr., if her husband's mother is alive; or Mrs. George Smith if he has an elder brother married. If the lady is the wife of the Honble. William Blunt, address her as the Honble. Mrs. Blunt. In addressing gentlemen or unmarried ladies who are "honourables", no other form is right. The Honble. William Blunt or the Honble. Enid Blunt is correct. When the Honble. Enid Blunt marries plain Mr. Jackson, she becomes the Honble. Mrs. Jackson. In addressing an unmarried lady say, "Dear Miss Jones", or if this is too familiar, "Dear Madame". For other forms of address, less generally required, see *The Art of Letter Writing* in this series of books.

INVITATIONS, ACKNOWLEDGING.—Earlier in this book, in the previous chapter, some particulars were given about writing invitations. These should always be accepted in a definite form: "Dear Mrs. Smith,—It is very good of you to ask me down for a week-end with you. I am sorry I shall be unable to reach —— before midday Saturday; my train arrives, or should arrive, about 12.45. I should like to get away early on Monday, to reach town by 10.30. I am looking forward to a good time. With kindest regards to yourself and Mr. Smith, Yours sincerely." Do not allow a letter to remain unanswered, whether an invitation or not.

INTRODUCTIONS, LETTERS OF.—These should always be given to the user unsealed, so that he may see what has been said, though it is more courteous to read the letter to him before it is handed to him. Leaving it unfastened signifies to the recipient, too, that the bearer is aware of the contents. If a letter of introduction is not used, it should be returned to the giver with a little note explaining the reason for its non-use.

ENCLOSURES.—If you send a letter to one individual to be forwarded to another, enclose a stamp. You should not put to pecuniary loss, even to this extent, one from whom you ask a courtesy. In sending a letter to a person unknown to you, when asking for information enclose a stamped addressed envelope for reply.

Although this is a very short chapter, it is an important one. There are probably more mistakes made in correspondence than in any other direction.

FOREIGN WORDS AND PHRASES.—In writing, do not air your knowledge of a foreign language or quotations from the classics. If your friend does not know their meaning, it will look as though you were trying to show off at another's expense.

PAGING.—If you must write on the pages in any other order than that in which they naturally run, number each page at the top. It is annoying to your correspondents to find that they cannot easily follow the letter. Do not cross the lines of writing. Even in wartime paper is cheap enough for this to be avoided. Let your writing be small, and you will get a lot of it on a sheet.

CHAPTER VIII

Love, Courtship, and Marriage

THAT happy and exacting period which precedes the more settled conditions of matrimony—the period which includes falling in love and the duration of the engagement—is one that calls particularly for restraint. A well-bred person does not wear his or her heart upon the sleeve. Not only are the emotions of love and joy too sacred to be openly discussed with outsiders, but one should always remember that others are not in that special, ecstatic condition. They will, naturally, appear interested. But they must not be expected to display excitement and ravishment when they are told of all the perfections of the loved one.

Do not trifle with the affections. For a man or woman to pretend that they are in love so as to lead the other on is contemptible. Many lives have been ruined in this way. Be straightforward, honest, and above-board in all that you do or say. If it appears that your conduct is misunderstood, that the little courtesies you are paying are taken to indicate something deeper, make an early opportunity to show that this is not so. Friendships between the sexes rapidly ripen into something warmer, and unless one is prepared to go on, care should be exercised.

Fortunately for all concerned, there is now much less sentimentality than formerly. Young men and young women meet and mix with one another much more freely than heretofore. This in itself is helpful. Girls are not so prone to believe that ordinary attentions mean anything more than their due. And young men find that girl friends are made and retained if they so desire.

Marriages are not made now at so early an age, and this, in some respects, is for the good of all concerned. It gives better opportunities to both to satisfy themselves that the partnership they propose to enter is a suitable one. Looks and dress count for less than formerly. It is qualities of head and heart that count the most. And so there is less "falling in love" haphazard and more of a steady friendship gradually assuming a warmer tone.

Although it is not in all cases customary for a man to ask the parents' consent to become engaged to the girl of his choice, it is still a becoming courtesy to ask her father before actually giving a ring and making an engagement binding. A parent has a great responsibility to a daughter, and it is his duty to see that her future husband is in a position to offer her a home and maintain her when necessary in suitable surroundings. It is evident, therefore, that before a man should approach a girl with an offer of marriage he should have some definite prospects with which to back up his offer.

Marriages are rarely childless—they should not be—and no man should wish to engage the affections of a girl if he has no early possibility of consummating their joint happiness in a home of their own. If he really loves the girl, he will see that he is spoiling her chances in life by a long engagement. For he is not the only pebble on the beach.

Love in a cottage is a delightful idyll. But even in a cottage rent and rates have to be paid. And it is *not* so easy to provide for two as one. Then, too, there are always things to be replenished, to say nothing of further little mouths to be fed. It is difficult to fix a standard of course. The mode of living varies in every walk of life; and what looks like poverty in the way of income to one individual is quite sufficient to maintain in comparative comfort others with simpler tastes, needs, and desires.

When engaged, it is not usual for young people to spend much time alone together. In some circles this is considered quite bad form. In other and simpler circles, it is taken for granted that young persons will like to be alone. In the company of others, engaged individuals should afford each other as much freedom as possible. There should be no expressed or implied desire to keep at one another's elbows all the time. The happy man should be pleased to see other men pay reasonable attentions to the woman who will grace his household later on. The girl, too, should be pleased to see her future husband paying courtesies to others of her own sex. He is honouring her through them.

Marriage is for both the beginning of a new life. For a time it may be a little heaven on earth of bliss. But let both beware how they awaken from this ecstatic dream. Marriage is for better or worse. And it may not be long before little tiny clouds arise in the sky. The married couple need have no fear; the sky will be bright again; clouds soon pass. But they should ever remember that it is the little courtesies from one to the other which are ever necessary, and which help to make the married state a happy union rather than a strained leash. Many men and many women, too, think that the smaller acts of courtesy may be omitted in their more familiar life. This is a great mistake.

The husband who crosses the room to open the door for his wife, who raises his hat to her when he meets her in the street, who never forgets the sweeter salute in the privacy of the household, is the one who holds his wife's affections the most closely. If anything, there should be a more scrupulous attention to these little courtesies.

Do not forget that your wife's letters, or your husband's letters, are not your concern. Usually, unless it be a matter of private business, the letter will be passed across for the other to read. But if not, it may be accepted that it is not anything that concerns more than the one individual. You would not expect to have the opportunity to see a private letter of someone else.

As far as possible, avoid the telling of little business or domestic troubles to the other. Each has his or her own sphere of work. There is no need to double trouble by relating it. On the other hand, take every opportunity to tell each other of the pleasant things that have befallen during the day. This is the way to double pleasure. Do not, above all, let the wife feel any economic dependence upon the husband. It is a partnership, and within reason, her duties being as responsible as the man's, she should share in the distribution of the income. It is a joint income, though, perhaps, only one appears to earn. The work of the wife in the home is no less important.

CHAPTER IX

Training the Children

MANY parents do not realise until perhaps rather late in life the enormous responsibility they incur in having children. It is borne in upon them when they have time to reflect upon the little deficiencies from which the children suffer and for which the parents are largely to blame.

IMITATION.—Children are remarkably imitative. One of their best and greatest games is to play at being grown up. In this can be seen how closely they observe their seniors, and how accurately they copy them. It is a safe rule to apply never to do or to say in the presence of your children what you would not wish them to say or do. As a positive rule, to balance the negative one above, be careful always to accentuate the points that matter when children are present. You may be sure that they will note it, and this will have its effect in after-life. If the children always see in the home life consideration and feeling for others displayed, they will early learn to do the same.

CHILDREN AND VISITORS.—Be careful how you inflict your children upon visitors to the house. However well-behaved children may be, they are apt to pall upon the visitor who has come to see you. This does not mean that children should be excluded altogether. They may come in, but should be instructed not to intrude unless asked to come, and to be ready to go at once as soon as a signal is given them.

CORRECTION OF CHILDREN.—When it is necessary to correct your children for some little misdemeanour or omission, try to make the correction positive rather than negative. To be continually saying to a child, "Don't do this", "Don't do that", emphasises to the childish mind the wrongdoing. It is quite as easy to suggest just what should be done. "Don't slam the door" is far better rendered, "Close the door quietly, dear." And when, perhaps, the children get noisy, as all children do, don't scold them for making a noise, but suggest some game to them that will insure more quiet.

GOOD-NIGHT AND GOOD-MORNING.—Children should be taught to bid all the members of the family good-night when retiring and good-morning when they meet at the beginning of another day. Little courtesies like these are apt to be overlooked, and then other delinquencies follow. On the other hand, if such courtesies as those mentioned are always practised, they are suggestive of others.

ANSWERING CORRECTLY.—Teach your children to speak out plainly and boldly when asked a question. But let them understand that they should wait to express an opinion until it is asked for. Two somewhat disagreeable traits that very many children exhibit are this failure to answer promptly and courageously any inquiry put to them, and the other type who are overbold and pert, who volunteer information, or even advice, unsought.

PUNISHMENT.—If it is really necessary to punish a child, do it with care and discrimination. A well-brought-up child should need very little actual punishment, for any offence will generally be due to exuberance of spirits or childish lack of thought and care. Remember always that a child is not an adult; that a child cannot have the experience of an adult, and errs mainly because the situation is a new one to it.

NEATNESS AND CLEANLINESS.—Lack of both these qualities is almost always a sign of inattention to growing children. They do not become orderly and nice in habits unless the wisdom of this is shown to them and insisted upon. Inculcate habits of order when they are quite young, by showing them how much easier it is to find toys and playthings that are put away where they may always find them when wanted again. Show them how dirty fingers spoil a clean suit or frock, and entail waste of time from play or walking out, because they must be changed.

CHILDREN AND SERVANTS.—Your own example should be enough to show your children how to treat those in a different position to yourself. But if you notice the children betraying any lack of consideration for inferiors, they should be shown how unkind this is, and how such conduct reacts upon themselves.

SITTING DOWN AND RISING.—Children should be instructed not to seat themselves in the presence of their seniors unless told to do so, or unless the others are seated. Boys should always rise when anyone enters the room, and should offer a chair if this be necessary.

INTERRUPTIONS AND NOISES.—It is necessary usually to caution young people about violent interrupting of their seniors. Something may have occurred to the boy or girl that is very interesting, and, perhaps naturally, they wish to tell others of it. But it may not be opportune just then to rush in and begin to talk. They should be told to wait for a suitable opportunity. It is pleasant to hear a boy whistle or a girl sing, but it is not always desirable that either of them should do so when their elders are near.

EATING AND DRINKING.—It is a necessary part of the training of children to see that they eat nicely, not too much, nor too frequently. Sweetmeats are good, but they should be allowed with discrimination. If not, children begin to think that they may have them at all times. This merely deranges the appetite. At table they should be taught to observe all the little points that have been put forward in the early part of this book.

MANLINESS.—Teach your boys to be honest in all things; never to do a mean or dirty action; to be straightforward and truthful in all their dealings; to be open, fearless, and courteous on all occasions, and especially to their sisters.

MODESTY.—Teach your girls to be as good as your boys (as fearless, as open, and as courteous), only from them a little more fineness and more reserve is expected—a tribute to their more delicate and finer nature.

Index

**A practical, sensible, concise guide to
The Art of Letter Writing.**

Unsure how to break off an engagement, accept an invitation to a country house weekend, complain about a courier or write to a countess? *The Art of Letter Writing* gives more than fifty examples of the perfect letter for any occasion, with numerous elegant and nuanced examples covering every possible social scenario. Filled with timeless advice and charming historical detail, this book is the perfect gift for anyone who has ever struggled to write a letter, offering encouragement and amusement alike.

Available at all booksellers, and at
www.bodleianbookshop.co.uk
ISBN: 978-1-85124-397-6
£7.99

LAYING THE FOUNDATION
STONE OF A NEW BLOCK
OF FLATS